THE
BOY
WHO
SAW
DOUBLE

20.7.20

THE
BOY
WHO
SAW
DOUBLE

20.7.20

WORK HARD NETWORK

DONNA J. KNIGHT

Cover by Donna J. Knight
Back cover author photo by Mary Redman

THE BOY WHO SAW DOUBLE
Copyright © 2020 by Donna J Knight
Published by WORK HARD NETWORK
Print Book ISBN 978-1-8380109-1-1
eBook Editions ISBN 978-1-8380109-0-4
Published by WORK HARD NETWORK

Editors: Aliya Hope Henry and Taé-Chan Rose Ellis.
Printed by www.beamreachuk.co.uk. United Kingdom.

CONTENTS

INTRODUCTION

It was always my dream to play collegiate basketball. At the age of nineteen, having been awarded a 4-year sports scholarship, I travelled to North America to study and play basketball at a private university. Little did I know that this opportunity would introduce me to a key and fundamental faith-based relationship that I would later come to rely on; not only to navigate my way through life, but to navigate my way through the most challenging experiences of life.

My experiences in basketball extended beyond being a successful student-athlete at university in America, as just prior to graduation I was called-up to represent the England Senior Women's Basketball team. This was the start of many trips out to represent my country.

FAST FORWARD, BECOMING A MUM

Prior to conception and becoming a mum to four children I had a vision, I had a vision that my children would follow in my footsteps, play basketball and like me travel to America on sports scholarships. The rationale behind my thinking being that from an early age, I would instil in my children a deep understanding of *the relationship between working hard and being successful.* My belief being that the skill set developed through sport is parallel to the skill set required to be successful in life.

My dream of my children developing a love for sport came to fruition, although much to my dismay their passion for sport was not for basketball. My third child Rashard entered the world with an exceptional gift for tennis, a sport I knew very little about. My limited understanding and knowledge of tennis did not bring disadvantage, because Rashard's gift knew no barriers, boundaries or limits. At age nine, on winning his first Surrey County Closed, he had his first experience of *the relationship between working hard and being successful.* Rashard had big dreams of going onto win championships, such as: Roland-Garros and Wimbledon, and because of his mindset, we believed that this vision was achievable.

FAST FORWARD, THE BOY WHO SAW DOUBLE

At the age of eleven, while attending tennis school and showing great signs of excelling in his chosen sport, Rashard developed double vision. A trip to the opticians saw us immediately being directed to the accident and emergency room at our local hospital. In hospital Rashard was diagnosed with Diffuse Intrinsic Pontine Glioma (DIPG). He had a tumour on his brain, which was inoperable. We were told he only had months to live.

I guess here is where the need to share our journey begins....

DEDICATION

This book is dedicated to my son, the late Rashard Miles Henry aka "THE BOY WHO SAW DOUBLE."

Through you God gave us insight and vision far beyond life. From a very early age you lived a life that challenged, motivated and inspired others. Your view and your perspective on life was incredible; your God given strength, self-belief and tenacity taught us all so much. For you not even the sky had limits. In the words of my dying son, "don't worry Mum I can still win Championships on that big tennis court up there in the clouds." The late Maya Angelou once said, "When you learn, teach. When you get, give." I write this book in the hope that I teach others what God taught me through you.

Son, you were wise beyond your years and you taught us so much in what seemed like a relatively short space of time. God sent you here with purpose and I am so grateful that you were able to live a life that allowed you to fulfil your purpose.

Ultimately, I am thankful that you were able to see and live out God's Will in a way that allowed and continues to allow you to touch, motivate and inspire the lives of others. The late Abraham Lincoln once said, "In the end it is not the years in your life that count. It is the life in your years."

Rashard you believed your purpose was to 'Work Hard' and to 'play tennis', but son your purpose proved to be so much more. Your journey was of strength, courage, determination and inspiration.

ACKNOWLEDGEMENTS

Thank you God for giving me the space to reflect on the gift and journey of life. Thank you for allowing me to follow you and lean on you through the ups and downs of this journey. Taking the time to reflect has given me a deeper insight and understanding into how you strengthened and prepared me for what was to come without me even realising. Thank you for teaching me that my blessings and challenges all require your presence. My soul is filled with your spirit. Developing an understanding that I can turn to you and lean on you from the inside out has been empowering; there is no doubt that my relationship with you and you alone was the foundation that kept me sane and focused through some very difficult and challenging times; the biggest challenge of all being to let go and say goodbye to my son. Through my son I came to know and truly understand that *pain is temporary, but eternal life is forever.* Thank you for the vision and insight that leads me to eternal life.

"For God so loved the world that He gave His only begotten Son, that whoever believes in Him shall not perish, but have eternal life." ~ John 3:16 [NIV]

Thank you for your deliverance and touching many lives through sharing your spirit through our son Rashard Miles Henry. To be chosen to be his Mum is such an honour and a blessing. There was darkness, sadness and pain in saying goodbye, but the joy and happiness of Rashard's presence in my life will always be my shining light.

"Again, Jesus spoke to them, saying, I am the light of the world. Whoever follows me will not walk in darkness but will have the light of life." ~ John 8:12 [ESV]

To my mum, I thank you for showing me from an early age how to be strong, survive and achieve in life. The past few years have been challenging for you, but as you know challenges can only make you stronger and more spiritually connected.

To my children, thank you for your support and encouraging me to 'work hard' to get your brother's book finished. Let us continue to work together to make Rashard proud.

Thank you to my family and friends for smiling with us through the fun times and praying with us during the most challenging times. Even in death I stand by the power of prayer and the fact that God's work is amazing.

Thank you to our Tennis Family; to the coaches, parents and children at Tennis Avenue, thank you for supporting us through this journey. Thank you for allowing Rashard to continue to live his dream through the difficult times. For all of you, we will forever be grateful. Hareen and Ilge, it was not always easy, but with your support Rashard was able to live out what he believed to be his purpose through tennis right up to the very end.

INTENTION

My intention for writing this book is to share the incredible journey of losing my son to Diffuse Intrinsic Pontine Glioma (DIPG). Recognising and realising the gift and teachings of my son through his presence in our lives, albeit for a short time, far outweighed the loss of him. For me the recognising and realising through reflection, that life is predestined prepared me for the passing of my son in a way that others may or may not understand.

My hope in writing this book and sharing our journey is that you are able to take a moment to pause and start to reflect on your own life experiences and journey. Taking time to revisit events that played out in your life and through reflection help you come to a realisation that there are some life experiences that you had and will continue to have absolutely no control over. Like me, you will come to gain a deeper understanding of the hand that an omnipresent God played out in your own life. For me the 'Aha' moments really helped me to put the passing of my son into perspective. I feel like I have finally been given some insight into events and experiences in my life that were all part of what I now come to know, acknowledge and accept to be part of *my predestined journey.*

In my book I share real life experiences that will provoke thought around predestination, omniscience and omnipresence. It will demonstrate how faith, knowing and trusting in God kept me free from burden and worry. I will introduce life experiences through story telling that unconsciously, but authentically on God's part prepared me for life. The biggest teaching for me in my teenage years was being introduced to a deeper and more meaningful relationship with God and the power of prayer; which for me came through basketball. God sent me 'Basketball Angels' for whom I will forever be grateful. Through basketball I unconsciously developed a deep and meaningful relationship with God; this relationship being the sole reason I believe why my heart and soul continue to smile beyond the passing of my son Rashard Miles Henry.

QUESTIONS:

Can you identify the point(s) in your life at which you developed a personal and meaningful relationship with God? What led you to the development of a spiritual relationship?

Are you able to identify and acknowledge that some of your trials and tribulations were an attempt to take you off course from your spiritual growth and personal relationship with God, and that these experiences were in fact lessons?

Do you give thanks to God and express gratitude for the knowledge and understanding gained in both the high and low points of your life?

On a scale of 0 to 10 how much control do you believe you have had on events that have played and continue to play out in your life?

0	1	2	3	4	5	6	7	8	9	10

TASK:
Throughout reading this book I would like to encourage you to take breaks and jot down notes of life experiences that immediately resonate with you. When you have a moment, go back and reflect on what you learnt from these experiences and if they linked to later life experiences:

• What did you learn from these experiences?
• Did any of these experiences teach you about what was to come later in your life journey?
• Were there any moments or events in your life where things were so big (too overwhelming) for you to process on your own that you automatically gave them to God to process on your behalf?

REFLECTIONS

REFLECTIONS

Chapter 1

TAKING TIME FOR REFLECTION

Reflection – "Careful or long consideration of thought" or
"Mental concentration; careful consideration."

R *eflection is a powerful tool.* When we take time to look back
at our life experiences and recognise through realisation
that our God is all-knowing and all-present we get what are
often referred to as 'Aha' moments.

We begin to realise that the burdens we once carried were not
ours to be carried, but instead lessons that were put before us
to prepare us for this journey called life. *A life that for the most
part can only be described as predestined.*

Taking time to reflect, recognise and realise the omnipresence
of an omnipotent and benevolent God is both *freeing* and
empowering. We begin to realise that there are no trials or
tribulations that our Maker cannot carry us through. The

beauty of omniscience is that God knows what is both in front of us and behind us. He knows what has already happened in our lives and what is about to happen; God knows what is in store for us, for it is already written and He knows our purpose.

> *"For I know the plans I have for you," declares the Lord, plans to prosper you and not to harm you, plans to give you hope and a future." ~ Jeremiah 29:11 [NIV]*

The ability to apply the knowledge and understanding of an all-knowing God into our daily lives through reflection is a *game changer.* Game changing moments that I was first introduced to through basketball. It amazes me just how much my basketball teaching and learning experiences can be linked to my spiritual journey through life; almost parallel if you like. Pausing and taking time to connect with the Holy Spirit, in silent communication, namely 'prayer' at any moment or time throughout the day will set you free. Life burdens and stresses will disappear, and if not fully disappear, you will feel lighter. Again, the power of prayer being one of the most important teaching and learning experiences that I gained through basketball. Just like winning and losing in basketball, recognising and realising that our past and present victories, trials and tribulations can only prepare us for what God already has planned for our future is freeing.

"So do not fear, because I am with you; do not be dismayed, for I am your God. I will strengthen you and help you; I will uphold you with my righteous hand." ~ Isaiah 41:10 [NIV]

Life's challenges can be so intense that they feel like battles. When we begin to acknowledge, accept and let go of what we perceived to be life challenges, we start to move through life lightly, stress-free, less anxious and without burden. It is in accepting that these experiences are all part of us living out our purpose which allows us to move on; this notion is isolated around predestination.

"Cast your burden on the LORD, And He shall sustain you; He shall never permit the righteous to be moved." ~ Psalm 55:22 [NKJV]

We begin to realise that there are many things in life that we actually have no control over. My eldest son Kaleed, since the passing of his younger brother Rashard has always preached 'predestination'. Letting go of situations that we once mentally and physically believed we had control over and surrendering all to God is the most incredible freeing feeling we will ever encounter.

The ability to develop a personal relationship with God and apply this knowledge and understanding to our daily lives is empowering. To know that our souls are filled with the Holy Spirit and that we can survive and celebrate from the inside out is incredible; allowing the burdens and turmoil that many people often sit with or carry unnecessarily to be lifted.

QUESTIONS:

Do you actively take time for daily reflection and to build on your spiritual relationship with God?

Do you actively practice gratitude daily?

How often do you take the time to say thank you? Not only to God, but to the people that you are fortunate to have in your life.

Do you need to build time into your day for silent reflection to express gratitude and appreciation?

TASK:

Create a time in your day that you can commit to taking ten to fifteen minutes for personal development and growth through spiritual reflection. My suggestion is that you do this first thing in the morning or last thing at night.

During Rashard's illness I would often find myself tired from meeting the demands of everyday life that came on top of nursing a sick child. The best piece of advice that I was given by a complete stranger was to lay in my bed in the morning, raise my hands up high and say, " God fill me with your spirit, fill me with you." Imagine taking the time each day to recharge your soul with the Holy Spirit, the only spirit that can truly strengthen and sustain you. It is a truly invigorating experience and I would recommend it to everyone.

> *"The LORD is my light and my salvation: Whom shall I fear? The LORD is the strength of my life; Of who shall I be afraid?" ~ Psalm 27:1 [NKJV]*

Remember there is nothing to stop you from pausing at low points during the day to recharge your soul. Just simply pause, stand still, raise your hands up above your head and say out loud "Lord fill me with you," you will literally feel the energy pass through your finger tips and travel down into your body. The energy generated through the Holy Spirit is incredible.

Equally, pausing at high points throughout the day to give thanks and show gratitude to the Holy Spirit circulating within you is just as important. A quick praise and a quick smile in recognition of joyful moments throughout the day is of equal importance. For me the song that often pops into my mind when I want to give thanks is *Lord I lift your name up high, Lord I love to sing your praises.*

REFLECTIONS

REFLECTIONS

Chapter 2

POWERING THROUGH ADVERSITY; INNER STRENGTH

Adversity – "A state or instance of serious or continued misfortune."

Resilience – "The capacity to recover quickly from difficulties; toughness."

There is something very powerful about a resilient mind that is able to adapt and make adjustments to overcome adversity. It is a well-known fact that the ability to push through adverse situations make you stronger. I spent hours and years on and off the basketball court in training, being pushed by my coaches and teammates to achieve goals that I would never have managed to accomplish on my own. Returning from summer break to run the sub 7-minute mile helped train and condition my mind into believing that I could achieve, which on the surface may first have appeared or felt impossible. Being pushed through limits and enduring what might feel like excruciating periods of suffering and pain can be life changing; especially when you are able to recognise and celebrate even the smallest of victories. There is an old saying, "God will not give you more than you are physically and emotionally able to handle." Being able to push through barriers and limitations that are sometimes perceived to be impossible, until tried, tested and achieved, should be celebrated as monumental moments through recognition and praise. It is no secret that personal development and growth come from adverse situations, trials and tribulations. In life we learn from our biggest loses just as much as we celebrate and learn from our biggest wins.

A mind that fully understands that there are no situations or circumstances that God, our maker, cannot push or pull us through, if we have faith and trust in him; known through 'Christianity' or if you prefer 'Spirituality' is worthy of praise and worship. For many of us, it is not until we are faced with difficulty and painful life experiences that we can truly appreciate and understand the power that lay in the personal relationship we have with God.

> *"Consider it pure joy, my brothers and sisters, whenever you face trials of many kinds, because you know that the testing of your faith develops perseverance. Allows perseverance [to] finish its work so that you may be mature and complete, not lacking anything." ~ James 1:2-4 [NIV]*

The mental, physical and spiritual strength that God gives to those of us who trust in him, during some of the most difficult times in our lives, experiences that might overwise break us without belief, is incredible. There is no greater feeling than being able to let go and give our troubles, anxieties and burdens to God.

My faith blossomed through adversity. The more I went through the more I turned to God. I literally let go and 'gave to God' total control over Rashard's experience with DIPG. I chose to trust that God would lead my family through this experience and that we would come out on the other side stronger no matter what the outcome. When you are in a situation that you realise you have absolutely no control over you have two choices, you either drown in burden or you walk in faith. I actively chose to walk in faith and my choice to walk in faith set the tone for my family. We were able to continue to live our day to day lives relatively anxious-free.

> *"do not be anxious about anything, but in everything by prayer and supplication with thanksgiving let your request known to God. And the peace of God, which surpasses all understanding will guard your hearts and your minds in Christ Jesus." ~ Philippians 4:6-7 [ESV]*

On reflection, prayer and supplication gave me an insurmountable strength that allowed me to travel through the assignment of living with DIPG with grace and dignity. God is faithful and, in my heart, I knew that God would eventually lead me out of what he led me into. The experience was far from comfortable, but I guess that was one of the challenges; to continue to trust God when walking through the unknown. This experience I recognised from the very beginning, was not just about Rashard and my family. I very quickly realised that the way in which we responded to the challenge of living with DIPG would set the tone for how other people would respond to their own life challenges and experiences.

> *"Praise be to the God and Father of our Lord Jesus Christ, the Father of compassion and the God of all comfort, who comforts us in all our troubles, so that we can comfort those in any trouble with the comfort we ourselves received from God." ~ 2 Corinthians 1:3-4 [NIV]*

QUESTIONS:

Have you faced periods in your life of high anxiety or been met with adverse situations?

Are you able to identify the people or forces that you turned to during difficulty?

Do you have any experiences that you can reflect on that will help you to recognise the power that lays in a spiritually resilient mind?

Are you able to reflect on experiences from early childhood which helped build your resilience?

I have often heard people use the phrase "trust in the process." Have you ever reflected on who you are really turning to and placing your trust in during the process?

Later on, throughout this book I will share some stories about how, through basketball, I further developed my spiritual resilience and learnt to bounce back through challenging times. My biggest resilience I now understand, being able to turn to and trust in God during both the high and low points travelled in my life. I, like many of you who are involved in sport, have been through pre-season trainings where I have said to myself "enough is enough, can we just get on with the season." Moments that I would later understand were part of my preparations for my later life experiences.

HOW DO WE GET OUR RESILIENCE FROM GOD?

For me resilience requires strength and for me I am able to recognise that my strength comes from God, the Holy Spirit which fills me. Sometimes God sends me on missions that I believe I could do without, only to realise that I have to surrender to God's will and to His way.

REFLECTIONS

REFLECTIONS

Chapter 3

WILDERNESS AND WONDER

Wilderness – "A wilderness experience" is often linked to a
   "mountaintop experience"; that is, the struggle follows a
   success of some kind. The period of trial comes on the
   heels of a period of accomplishment or achievement."

Wonder – "A feeling of amazement and admiration, caused
   by something beautiful, remarkable and unfamiliar."

God used basketball to lead me into the *wilderness* and He
kept me there based on *wonder*. The success of basketball
being my *'mountaintop experience'* that would unexpectedly lead
me into unknown territory. As a reward for my successes in
basketball, God led me into what felt like one of the most
remote corners of the world. Preparation for a range of
different experiences that would later follow in my life;
the death of my son to DIPG being the major of these
experiences. The curiosity and wonder that I developed as

I travelled through the darkness of the wilderness, cast light on and illuminated the path that I travelled. At first the light was dim, but the deeper I got into the wilderness and started to understand my teachings, the brighter the light would glow. I have many stories of success of which I experienced while traveling through the wilderness. Through my travels there was always light, even on roads that sometimes felt like darkness.

Through basketball God led me into isolation; He took me to a 'foreign land' that at times led me to question if I had been teleported into a whole new realm. The feeling of removal from my life at the time, into a new life, hit me so deep that I can vividly remember having a dream that I had been shot dead and entered a new world. On reflection this dream seems very symbolic. God moved me from the comforts of my familiar and known surroundings of home in London, England to the remote unknown and unfamiliar grounds of Nampa, Idaho. He isolated me from an unforgiving world long enough for me to deeply internalise his teachings.

The purpose for isolation, I now understand was so God could safely strip back my soul to reveal to me a hollowness that would exist in my life if not filled and generated by the Holy Spirit.

God used the guise of basketball to cast me into an area where Christianity was and still is the foundation of All-being. He not only cast me into a new world, but he ensured that

I crossed paths and developed some deep and meaningful faith-based relationships with believers that would positively influence, shape my perspective, and understanding about life. He introduced me to my coaches who would challenge me to teach me the importance of the relationship between working hard and being successful. He introduced me to the Courseys' and the Whittingers' who modelled good faith-based core family values. These families strengthened me with virtues such as kindness, courage and working together. They taught me the importance of sharing and that all God's children, known or unknown, are worthy of acceptance and love. He introduced me to professors who showered me with a fountain of knowledge. They taught me valuable information from a Christian perspective, but worldly enough that I could survive when I returned into a world in which I would cross paths with 'non-believers'.

Through basketball I met my sister Mary. We were a force to be reckoned with on the court and this set the standard for the force others were going to come to reckon with as we entered adult life. Mary is a believer that God kept in my life for accountability. From a distance we do life together. The biggest piece of life that we continue to do together is in relation to God. Since graduating, Mary would always send me bible verses or direct me to sermons that she knew would speak directly to my heart. You see our lives are so similar that we often joke about living in a parallel universe. When it looked like I was starting to wither my sister sent me a bible in the post. She knew that I needed to spend more time with our

Maker if I was to successfully complete this mission relatively unscathed. What God showed me through Mary was that he will always send the army that you require to give you encouragement and strength when needed.

My unawareness of God's spiritual teaching and intention, through basketball, meant that it in fact took me twenty-eight years to travel through and find my way out of a wilderness experience that could have possibly taken just four years. I put the fact that my journey took seven times longer than expected, down to my lack of obedience and understanding surrounding the purpose of this mission. Remember, my belief was that I was going to America to become a better basketball player and to earn a college degree, both of which I successfully achieved. I had no idea that the critical teachings and core foundation of my collegiate basketball experience was going to be Christ-centred.

I do not believe that God intended or anticipated that it would take me so long to find my way out of the wilderness, but I acknowledge that the journey took longer due to disobedience, temptation and from time to time straying off path. God himself put no time limit on me finding my way out of the wilderness, but what he did do is strengthen my character through his children that I met along the way, to ensure that I would eventually find my out.

QUESTIONS:

Are you able to identify your mountaintop experience?

Are you able to identify your wilderness experience?

Can you identify and link the two experiences?

Has God ever enticed you into a situation through showing you something you love, only to realise that he used what you love to show you what you needed to see?

Can you recall times in your life where you have strayed off path through stubbornness and disobedience?

Has an idea or goal taken you longer to achieve because you did not take the time to look at a path that God was so very clearly showing you?

REFLECTIONS

REFLECTIONS

Chapter 4

BASKETBALL ANGELS

Angel – "A spiritual being believed to act as an attendant, angel, or messenger of God, conventionally represented in human form with wings and a long robe."

God introduced me to my 'Basketball Angels', Coach T, Coach C and Coach G in preparation for my journey through life. God used these three wise men to open doors of opportunity, through which Christ would lead me closer to God. My 'Basketball Angels' taught me a fundamental skill set that echoes life. To me they demonstrated the importance of supporting and helping others to develop and embed skills that would later be necessary for me to apply, in order for me to navigate my way through life.

Coach T. From the very beginning he was like a father figure to me and my junior teammates. From the start he taught us that we could be successful, regardless of our background or where we came from. He gave us an unbelievable level of self-belief and confidence. We just had to be willing to work hard if we wanted to achieve. There were days when we were not always willing to work hard, but Coach T had a stubbornness and determination, led by a deep level of patience and kindness that meant he was going drill his philosophy into our heads until it became second nature. It was not easy for Coach T, but his determination I now understand, stemmed from his own life experiences.

He had high expectations of us both on and off the basketball court and he held us accountable on meeting these expectations until they became embedded to the point that they became our self-expectations.

Coach C. I will never forget the day that I met Coach C. He was literally a God send. The answers to my prayers. You see, I was ambitious in basketball and had always dreamt of going to America on a Basketball Scholarship, I just did not know how.

One summer, a Christian basketball travelling team came to London. It just so happened that this team ended up playing my Junior basketball team at the local youth centre.

I can remember half time of the game against the team like it was yesterday. It was during this time that the travelling players gave testimonies of their lives and how they came to know God. I was intrigued by the narratives that these young players were able to stand up and share. Their testimonies immediately touched my heart and my soul.

At the end of the evening Coach C came over to introduce himself to me. He did not talk about the fact that I had just played a great game, but he spoke to me about my eyes and how he had observed me listening with intent to the testimonies shared at half time. I believe he was the only person that evening that saw how this 'basketball game' was about to play out in my life.

Coach G. A year after meeting Coach C and following my team taking up an invite to attend a basketball camp in Seattle Washington, I was introduced to Coach G. This introduction would see me arrive in Nampa, Idaho with the expectation that I would play high school basketball for a year before going onto play collegiate basketball, but our all-knowing and ever-present God already aware of his own intentions, had other plans. Plans to lead me to attend a local Christian university.

QUESTIONS:

Are you able to reflect and think of times that you crossed paths with your own life angel(s)?

Are you able to identify and understand God's purpose in introducing you to these Angels?

What was your teaching and learning from your experience?

REFLECTIONS

REFLECTIONS

Chapter 5

PRAYER WARRIORS

Prayer – "A solemn request for help or expression of thanks addressed to God or another deity."

NORTHWEST NAZARENE COLLEGE, NOW KNOWN AS NORTHWEST NAZARENE UNIVERSITY:

On arrival to Nampa, Idaho I was very quickly introduced to Coach Schmidt and Coach Ely- more 'Basketball Angels'. They in turn would immediately introduce me to the importance and *power of prayer*; I guess they could both be described as 'Prayer Warriors'. Without a shadow of doubt, these two coaches introduced me to a whole new way of approaching basketball. They tested me in ways that I did not know that I could be tested, both on and off the court.

From the get-go Coach Schmidt introduced me to the harsh reality of what some of my wilderness experiences were going to teach me. He recently reminded me of a conversation I had at the start of my freshman year:

It felt like we had been practising for weeks, I had not heard any conversation about playing games or seen a schedule for the season. I approached Coach Schmidt: "Coach, when are we going to play games?" To my disappointment the answer was not what I wanted to hear. Coach Schmidt replied, "Donna, we have six more weeks of practice before we play our first game." I had a flashback in which I very quickly visualised the A5 note cards that he would methodically post on the wall at the start of each practice. Flashbacks of the exact point at which he would outline when we were going to run a sweet sixteen, on occasion back to back sweet sixteens', but if we were really lucky, we got to run suicides.

Coach Schmidt and Coach Ely would take any given moment or opportunity for prayer; they would pray at the end of each practice, before and after each game, win or lose, before we left for road trips and prior to us heading back from our road trips, prayers for our safe return or if our opponents came to Idaho, prayers for their safe return. Some of the snow on the roads in Idaho back then definitely required prayer. The fact that my basketball coaches were prayer warriors meant that prayer, without choice or a deeper level of understanding, very quickly became a part of my daily routine for four straight years. The important thing to note is that I was taught that prayer should not only be used to communicate with God during difficult and challenging times, when asking for guidance or answers, but should also be used during moments of celebration and to express gratitude. I had never been around so much prayer before going to Nampa, Idaho 'to play basketball'.

The art of prayer, a colourful method of communication that I would later come to know, understand and rely on as the most essential, faithful and trusted method of communication during both good and challenging moments in time; having an omnipresent God meaning that I can turn to him at any given moment.

Coach Schmidt and Coach Ely were shining examples of 'God fearing men,' a term I had not heard of or been questioned about before meeting Coach Ely. I can clearly remember at the start of my collegiate basketball career Coach Ely asking me whether or not I was God fearing. It was in my very early days at NNU, a period of time of uncertainty; not knowing if I had the strength or courage to withstand the unknown Christian territory of Northwest Nazarene University. To be totally honest, I was a little confused by Coach Ely's question, it felt like a trick question. I can remember thinking to myself, why couldn't he just ask me whether or not I believed in God? The answer would have been a simple yes.

The religious aspect of NNU life on occasion was quite intimidating, I was surrounded by coaches, teammates and college students that could quote bible verses at the drop of a hat. As part of the requirements to attend NNU we were required to go to Chapel two or three times per week. I can vividly remember the area that we claimed to be the basketball section in the church. It was at the back to the far left. Some days we would use our time in Chapel to study and prepare for tests and other days we would be captivated by great speakers, who we would tune in and listen to. By my senior and final year at NNU I found myself tuning more and more into the sermons that were being delivered. I began to have my favourite hymns. Hymns that are still my favourite to this day. It is these songs that I would later hum to myself or sing out loud in moments of trouble or moments of celebration.

QUESTIONS:

Who introduced you to the importance and power of prayer?

Do you understand the power of prayer?

Do you communicate with God through prayer during both difficult and celebratory moments in time or do you tend to lean towards prayer during one or the other of these moments?

REFLECTIONS

Chapter 6

THE BOY WHO SAW DOUBLE
AKA RASHARD MILES HENRY

Rashard Miles Henry born on December 28th, 2002, had a vision. He had a vision that he was going to be the best tennis player in the world. He also, from a very early age, understood that he was going to have to work hard to achieve his vision. Rashard from the get-go was very determined, and he was not afraid to openly declare that one day he was going to be number one in the ATP Rankings. The most incredible thing about what Rashard believed to be his life purpose, was that God blessed him with a soul of which embodied a spirit of which encompassed the skill set, sharpness, strength and determination required to work towards achieving his vision. The biggest gifts that God blessed Rashard with, specifically relevant to tennis, were a great mind and great hands. Nick, one of the tennis coaches that worked with Rashard while he was on the WJTI squads, described his gift simply and eloquently by saying, "Rashard had super hands, a real artist."

"God has given each of you a gift from his great variety of spiritual gifts. Use them well to serve one another." ~ 1 Peter 4:10 [NLT]

"Do you have the gift of speaking? Then speak as though God himself were speaking through you. Do you have the gift of helping others? Do it with all the strength and energy that God supplies. Then everything you do will bring glory to God through Jesus Christ. All glory and power to him forever and ever! Amen." ~ 1 Peter 4:11 [NLT]

On arrival into this world God also gifted Rashard with 'presence'. From a toddler, God blessed Rashard with a statute that resembled a childlike version of Muhammad Ali. There was no arrogance about Rashard, but yet his presence oozed confidence, strength, self-belief and determination. He had a soft, selectively-spoken, imposing presence with a powerful silent and confident demeanour about him. This make-up allowed Rashard to go about his business and to tackle tasks in a silent but confident way. Rashard carried a determined look in his eyes that spoke volumes without words.

Rashard had this very distinct level of courage and confidence, which I am aware on occasion others misinterpreted as stubbornness or arrogance, but those who knew Rashard well, knew that he did not have an ounce of arrogance in his body. Rashard's God given confidence allowed him to zone in and focus on fulfilling what he believed to be his sole purpose in life, this purpose being tennis. Rashard was so full of self-belief and an understanding of who he was, that he often struggled to understand why adults would attempt to impose their beliefs and interpretation of tennis and how he should play onto him; this left Rashard wondering why he or others were not being encouraged to just be themselves.

"But blessed is the one who trusts in the lord, whose confidence is in him." ~ Jeremiah 17:7 [NIV]

I am not sure how, but Rashard knew exactly who he was and who God sent him into this world to be. He did not allow others to impede upon his vision, or if you like God's vision and purpose for sending him into the world. I akin Rashard's presence to that of a prophet. On reflection it blows my mind to think about the power there is in knowing the purpose behind your being and acting on it, despite opposing forces. Imagine being so young, so focused and self-assured of who you are. Having a deep understanding of your purpose and the message you are sent to deliver and teach to others from such an early age is incredible, but even more incredible is reaching the realisation and understanding that such a presence can only be anointed by God our Maker. You have to truly be spiritually connected to function and operate at a level with such power and strength. Rashard was what I would term both 'chosen' and 'special'. He was without doubt guided and protected as he travelled along what often felt like a turbulent pathway in order to fulfil his purpose.

"I will instruct you and teach you in the way you should go; I will counsel you with my loving eye on you." ~ Psalm 32:8 [NIV]

Rashard was what was others often referred to as 'gifted' and for the most part, because of his diligence, he was successful in whatever he turned his hand to. He was always in the top sets for education and he was also a great athlete. Rashard had a calculating mind that got great joy from figuring things out for himself. The tennis courts I would describe as Rashard's biggest classroom. He loved to learn and to take risks when he was out on the tennis court. You could always tell when Rashard had figured something out because you would see him silently grin to himself.

QUESTIONS:

Has anyone ever limited your thinking by attempting to impose their ideas, opinions or beliefs on you about how you should live your life?

Have you ever been deterred from pursuing your goals, dreams and what you believe to be your purpose based on the opinions and influence of others?

Where do limitations come from? Do you understand that there cannot be limitations on what God has ordained you to do? God calls you to trust in him.

At what age were you able to articulate your vision and purpose in life?

Dream, goals or passion. Have you identified your purpose in life?

Do you believe that your God given purpose or calling has been revealed to you?

Are you following and living out your purpose or calling?
If yes, how does that make you feel? If no, what is holding you back from fulfilling what has been revealed to you and what you have identified as your purpose or calling?

It is important to note that not everyone is able to identify or articulate what they believe to be their purpose in life. I do, however, believe that every single one of us has a God given purpose. Often some people are deterred from living out or following what they believe to be their purpose because of anxiety and fear. Very often these anxieties and fear are projected into us by others.

Have you identified your passion in life? If yes, what is it?
If no, I want you to pause and think about what makes you feel most alive and happy. Write down 5 things that you enjoy doing in life. Arrange them in the order in which they bring you most joy.

We are all different. Some of us find joy in helping others. Some of us find joy in playing a sport or playing an instrument.

My question to you is, "What lights your fire? What makes you feel alive?"

REFLECTIONS

Chapter 7

NOW WAY OUT ~ PREDESTINED, PREMONITION OR BOTH?

Predestined – "(Of an outcome or course of events)
determined in advance by divine will or fate.
'Our predestined end'."

Premonition – "A strong feeling that something is about to
happen, especially something unpleasant."

There is a saying "every picture tells a story." Well who would have known that a picture which Rashard painted one year prior to being diagnosed with DIPG would be so powerful. You see, Rashard's class had been to visit some London art galleries and to finish the term each pupil was required to paint a picture of choice; Rashard chose to paint what I thought was a random picture of an eye being attacked by a fire breathing dragon. For his class art exhibition, he titled his painting 'NO WAY OUT!!!'. The description of his artwork that hung next to it very clearly explained what the picture represented. He also went as far as to write down the questions that he wanted people to ask themselves when viewing his painting.

To paint such a detailed picture of an eye, with a clear explanation was incredible. Although described as an artist on the tennis court, Rashard had never enjoyed or previously completed a piece of artwork in an 'art class' in his life. From an early age Rashard never found joy in drawing or colouring pictures, but for some reason this painting was completed with great detail. For me the picture could only be described as captivating and intriguing. In fact, I found the painting and its description thought-provoking to the point that I chose to hang it on the wall at home. This was the only piece of artwork I had ever put on display at home for any of my four children. I always liked to keep the walls at home plain white and minimal, it just kept the house clear and less chaotic, but for some reason I felt that this painting needed to be placed on the wall. I hung the artwork on the wall without further thought and did not go back to look at it until a year later following Rashard's DIPG diagnosis.

It is amazing to me because it was only at the point at which Rashard was diagnosed with DIPG that I gave second thought to the painting. In fact, it was thoughts of the mementos that I had of Rashard that led me to revisit the picture that I hung on the wall. As I approached the painting I had absolutely no recollection of what I was going to find. Yes, I had been so amazed by the picture to the point that I felt the need to hang it on the wall, but honestly if you had offered me a million pounds to tell you at that moment in time what Rashard had painted, I would have failed miserably. As I approached the painting, shock immediately ran through my body. I quickly reached for my mobile phone and called a work colleague that had become a friend. The fact that he shared a passion and interest in tennis is the reason our friendship developed. He would often come to watch my children train and work towards fulfilling their dreams of becoming the best tennis players in the world. The reason my first thought was to reach for my phone and contact my friend was because I had shared the painting and description with him on attending the original school art exhibition. I can remember him also being intrigued by Rashard's painting. At the time he had a discussion with a friend of his, who was an Educational Psychologist. She too was intrigued by the painting and at the time had said she would like to meet with Rashard to discuss his thought process behind the image that he produced. My work colleague at the time, laughed off her request and told me that it was best if we leave Rashard alone; so, at the time, alone we left him.

Calling my friend, I quickly asked him: "Do you remember the picture that Rashard painted last year? He paused for a moment; I could tell that everything came flooding back to him. "Oh yes, I remember the picture," he said. "It's an eye," I declared, "not only is it an eye, it's an eye under attack," I said. We then went on to talk in more detail about the picture and I read out the description. My friend very quickly and sarcastically pointed out that this picture was not a coincidence. I think we were both silently shocked by what we had uncovered that we finished the conversation and in our own way went away for deeper reflection.

The revelation and meaning behind the painting was made known to us on Wednesday 9th July 2014, this marks the day that would change our lives forever. Rashard had been suffering from double vision for a few weeks. Within that time, he had been prescribed glasses, but these glasses did not make any difference to Rashard's double vision.

We arrived at the opticians at exactly 9:20am. I remember the time so clearly because I parked in the Sainsbury's car park and had to keep track of my pay and display ticket. We walked up to the counter and explained that we needed an urgent appointment because we were travelling to America the next morning on urgent family business. I gave her an insight into why we were travelling in an attempt to get an immediate appointment. The reason we were traveling to America being that my Dad had suffered a big stroke on the Saturday before, and the hospital were awaiting our arrival before switching off the life support machine.

I explained my concerns in relation to Rashard's eyes with the belief that he just needed the prescription of his lens to be changed. The fact that we had been to a different optician two weeks earlier meant that the lady behind the counter tried desperately to accommodate us. Despite her efforts, she looked up and said, "sorry but we are extremely busy this morning," she went on to explain that if we went away and came back at 2:00pm she would be able to see Rashard. This was not really the news I wanted to hear because in my mind I still had so much left to do before we travelled to Florida the next morning. As the lady was telling us that she couldn't see Rashard, she proceeded to call the customer due to attend the 9:30am appointment. I tuned into the conversation quickly enough to understand that the person at the other end of the line was unable to keep the appointment. As the optometrist hung up the phone she said "great, fantastic I can do a thorough eye test right now because the appointment has just been cancelled." I can remember saying to myself "God is good." I believe that moments like these are referred to as 'divine intervention'. The optometrist tested Rashard's eyes thoroughly for one hour and twenty minutes, again I am reminded of the time because of where I had parked my car.

The one thing I will never forget is the way in which Rashard described in great detail the extent to which he was seeing double. I remember the moment so clearly because not only can I remember his detailed explanations of how he worked hard to alleviate the handicap of having double vision on the tennis court, but I can remember the fact that my heart sank and literally felt like it was going to drop out of my body. Rashard very meticulously and articulately described to the optometrist not only how he had been seeing double, but he equally played great attention to detail when he explained how he had calculated a way to overcome the double vision. A way that would allow him to continue to engage in playing the sport that he cared so passionately about. Rashard was able to explain that the double vision was not too much of a handicap at first because the balls originally appeared closer together, but over time the gap between the balls had widened and so this initially made it difficult for him to decide which, of what appeared to be two balls, to hit. He went on to explain that he found playing tennis most difficult with double vision when he was serving.

Rashard described in great detail, very similar in the way in which he painted his picture in great detail, not only how he had been getting double vision, but how he had worked out how to alleviate the double vision. Rashard demonstrated through a shadowing motion, using his arms and hands through the air to emulate a serving action. In the middle of the small eye testing room, Rashard demonstrated how he would toss the ball up to serve, he then continued his demonstration by explaining that as he tossed the ball up he would see two balls. Rashard not only meticulously described the problems that he encountered when trying to serve with double vision, but he very clearly explained the solution he had arrived at to overcome the challenge on seeing two balls when in reality there was only one. Rashard explained to the optometrist that in seeing two balls, he had worked out that if he hit the side of the outside of the outside ball he would make contact and get a lot of power on his serve. The next point of focus was to ensure that the ball landed on the inside of the correct service line. The difficulty in seeing two balls was only starting to hinder him because the double vision was causing the two balls to split further and further apart. It was now taking Rashard a split second longer to be able to see which ball to hit. I find it amazing how Rashard's eye-hand coordination managed to continue to operate with such precision under such time limited decision-making circumstances.

After one hour and twenty minutes of testing, the optometrist declared that we needed to go straight to A&E immediately. She explained that there was a nerve under Rashard's left eye that was not working and that this was linked to his brain. The optometrist hand wrote an A4 letter and said we needed to drop a copy into our doctor's surgery on the way to the hospital.

QUESTIONS:

What drew me to the painting after it had been hanging on the wall for one year?

What made Rashard paint that picture and write such a detailed description?

Have you ever had an experience where a picture or painting gave you insight or vision into a future event?

REFLECTIONS

REFLECTIONS

Chapter 8

DREAMING

Dream – "A series of thoughts, images, and sensations occurring in a person's mind during sleep."

There are three dreams that stand out in my mind in the run up to Rashard being diagnosed with DIPG. The first dream was a disturbing dream that I made a conscious decision to remove from my mind.

I dreamt that I was being told that there was something wrong with Rashard's brain, that literally, like a sharp shooter with a gun on target, aimed directly to his brain. It was as though the point at which the bullet was going to land, revealed to me the point at which this bullet was going to hit, although in reality the brain tumour was not an actual target for the bullet, it still yielded the same outcome. In my dream it was very clear that I was being told that Rashard had something terribly wrong at a single point in his brain. This was a very disturbing dream that immediately upon waking up shook me and led me to question why I would even have such a dream. I now know that this dream was a premonition about what was to come, and I also know that when you have such a revelation, that no matter how much you choose to ignore it, there is no getting away from it. As much as I chose to displace this dream in denial by immediately tucking it away, in what I felt was a safe place at the back of my mind, I have now learnt that such dreams cannot be removed from reality in this way.

This dream definitely unsettled me, but in that moment, I was able to pause, think about it and then immediately tuck it away; far away enough not to let it linger and bother me, but clearly close enough to remember that I had it. I had a choice given to me in this dream, I could go with Rashard or I could stay. In later revisiting this dream I was presented with a choice, me revisiting the dream, I want to add, was not by choice, but necessary as I had to make a choice. I chose to stay, to be here for my other children, as it seemed absurd that I would choose to leave them behind. Unlike my first dream, the second dream I could not tuck away in the same way.

The second dream was a reoccurring dream, I kept dreaming that Rashard and I were travelling downhill in a car. I was always driving and Rashard was always in the passenger seat. The dream followed the same pattern, I would be driving, Rashard would be in the passenger seat and I would lose control of the car, unable to break. I can vividly remember one time crashing into a low wall and ending up in the ocean.

There was nothing I could do to displace this dream because for a period of time it was reoccurring. I would always wake up puzzled and slightly worried about what it meant, but in reality did not acknowledge the significance of this dream and the fact that I was unconsciously being powerfully informed of the most significant event that was about to be played out in my life.

The third and final dream that I vividly remember and link to the time frame of being informed of what was to come, was a dream of me standing in my kitchen and someone lunging towards me to attack me with a knife. Rashard out of nowhere shielded me from the attack by placing his arm out and stepping across me, placing his body in front of me to protect me. Rashard clearly saved me, but my dream did not reveal what happened after that point. Until this day, thinking about this dream leaves me feeling rather emotional. The reason being that thoughts come to my mind around the possibility of my son cutting his life short in order to save me.

I try not to think about these dreams too often, but I have to be honest and say that these dreams were close to the front of my mind as we travelled through our journey of living with DIPG.

It may sound strange, but I do wonder if Rashard's life was cut short to make mine longer. No matter what my thoughts are around these dreams, I am at peace in knowing that I had literally no control over what was already written.

"For even the Son of Man came not to be served but to serve, and to give his life as a ransom for many." ~ *Mark 10:45 [NIV]*

"Greater love has no one than this, that someone lay down his life for his friends." ~ *John 15:13 [ESV]*

QUESTIONS:

Have you ever had a dream in which something was revealed to you?

Have you ever had a reoccurring dream?

If yes, would you count your dream as a vision into what we know as predestined or premonition, or both?

What are your thoughts and views around the fact that some dreams may give us insight into future events?

REFLECTIONS

Chapter 9

DIFFUSE INTRINSIC PONTINE GLIOMA

D*iffuse Intrinsic Pontine Glioma (DIPG)* is an inoperable brain tumour. These tumours are highly aggressive and difficult to treat because of the location in which they present. DIPGs are in the pons area of the brain- they are a brainstem glioma. These tumours are present in the bottom portion of the brain connecting the cerebrum with the spinal cord. DIPGs grow and spread through the nerves and this is why they are inoperable.

They grow in the area which controls breathing, blood pressure and heart rate. As DIPGS grow, they impact the ability to control body functions such as movement, breathing, swallowing and eye movement.

GOD SOMETIMES USES OTHER PEOPLE TO COMMUNICATE OR CONVEY A MESSAGE TO US:

It is never easy to hear that anyone you know has cancer, let alone your child. The harsh reality is that there is something worse than being told that your child has got cancer, being told that your child has terminal cancer that cannot be reached is pretty much indescribable. I would liken it to a 'knock-out blow' to your system, and your own lights very close to going out. Ah, but alas, who would have known that a knockout blow to the system could be counter punched by words shared through the mouthpiece of an oncologist. "Unimaginable," I hear people shouting from the rafters. "Impossible, how could the words of an oncologist sooth such a blow?" Well, believe me it is true, the words of Dr Z. filled me with both comfort and hope. In fact, before the words even left Dr Z.'s mouth, I felt like I was being thrown the biggest lifeline of my life; this experience is a reminder of how great and faithful Our Maker is.

I cannot explain the strength and power of God's timing to remind me of his presence. These words were not spoken by chance, they were spoken and directed by God. The day that we were told that Rashard had a 'rare' childhood brain tumour that affects, what we were told at the time, 1 in 600,000 children, is clearly a day that I will never forget. Hearing that the prognosis for children who receive such life changing and debilitating news is nine months maximum, can only be described as mind blowing. "No child has ever survived," Dr Z. an Oncologist at the time working at the Royal Marsden claimed, as he delivered the news in what seemed like very quick, short, sharp sentences. Yes, this news was devastating, but little did Dr Z. know that the final words of our conversation would be so powerful and determine the way in which I would lead my family and our approach to Rashard's DIPG diagnosis. Hearing Dr Z. finish with the words, *"but we are not God"* provided an unexplainable level of comfort at the end of what I can only describe as the most difficult conversation I have ever had to have in my entire life. The four words that rolled off of Dr Z.'s tongue *"We are not God"* and that "medicine changes daily" gave me an incredible feeling of hope. Dr Z.'s words touched my soul before they could even finish leaving his mouth. In that moment I was reminded that I am a child of God and that through it all, we would be guided and protected by the Lord God, our Maker.

For me, I now understand that God wanted to make it very clear to me that the burden and stress of what was to come was not mine to carry and that His omnipresence meant that I could take refuge in Him. It was also at this point that I knew and chose to recognise that everything about to come was going to be way beyond my control and ability to manage. It was in that said moment that I was reminded that all I needed to do was to give everything to God. Teachings that immediately resurfaced, internalised from my earlier introduction to the importance of a deep and much needed personal relationship with God our Father, and prayer. I do not know why, but I instantly knew that there was no way that

I was going to be able to care for Rashard and to look after my other three children without acknowledging and accepting that I would have to fully trust that God was ready to carry us all through this journey. As mentioned previously, there are times in life where you are going to have to make a choice between drowning in burden or walking in faith. Well in this moment, walking in faith was the only option.

It might sound weird, but if you speak to my friends and family that were on this journey with us, you will hear them talk about my strength. Little did many know or understand that it was not my strength, but the Holy Spirit of which God fills me, that carried and strengthened me through what would have otherwise completely destroyed me.

Dr Z.'s words immediately transported me straight back to the teachings that I had received and internalised during my time at Northwest Nazarene University. I knew who I needed to turn to, pray to and rely on at this time more than any other moment in my life. Yes, I had family and friends that would support me and that I would be able to visibly see day to day with my eyes, but the relationship I had unconsciously deeply internalised with God was far more powerful and went way beyond vision. I knew that God was the one person that I could truly trust, turn to, rely on and call upon from the inside out; I had faith that our omnipresent God could hear my cries and meet my needs at any given moment in time.

> *"and call upon me in the day of trouble; I will deliver you, and you shall glorify me." ~ Psalm 50:15 [ESV]*

The more and more I reflect on the message that could have floored me and literally knocked the spirt out of my soul, the more and more I am reminded of our Makers faithfulness. That old saying "God moves and speaks in mysterious ways" is what I can only describe as the truth. To be still and listen is very powerful.

> *"Be Still and Know That I am God." ~ Psalms 46:10 [NIV]*

> *"The LORD will fight for you, you need only to be still." ~ Exodus 14:14 [NIV]*

The moment that my son Rashard was diagnosed with DIPG is the moment that I had no choice, but to be still. Maybe I was momentarily paralysed by what I was hearing. I am truly grateful that the Holy Spirit that fills my soul went into autopilot; literally like a generator that kicks into action when the power goes out. On reflection it is so difficult to be able to describe exactly what happened, other than the feeling of knowing that God had me, which was comforting. I mean, how else could anyone describe God speaking those words through Dr Z. if he was not forever present? To be able to recognise and feel God's presence in my most challenging of times has truly changed the way I view life.

God's commitment to walk with or should I say carry me and lead me with the promise of deliverance, through this predestined journey called life, has truly changed my approach to overcoming any adverse situations that I may face in life. Life is fragile and it can take a turn at any moment. Yes, with Rashard's DIPG diagnosis there were moments that I would feel weak and shed tears, but I never really felt alone or the need to ask why. Other people would ask why or try to give me reasons why this should not have happened to Rashard but should have happened to another child. They would give examples of a troubled child or a child with what looked like less potential ahead of them, but in truth, the why never sat in me or with me. You see, I believe in Heaven and I know that it is a beautiful place. I refused to allow DIPG to take control of me or hold my mind hostage because in truth, only an all-knowing and all-powerful God can ever be fully in control of any situation that might arise in life. In my heart I knew that we as a family would be better equipped, able to cope and manage based on the fact that our courage and strength is built on a strong faith or if you like, a spirit filled foundation.

For the DIPG journey I chose to use the term 'living with cancer' when the oncologist announced that Rashard had a rare childhood brain cancer, called DIPG, and that the prognosis was 9 months max. I not only chose to look at ways that we could attempt to survive cancer, but I also chose to look at how we could continue to live life through this part of our predestined journey. I chose to live in hope rather than live in death. Vision and choice are important aspects of any of life's challenging learning experiences; vision very often based on and led by faith. There is no human being that can tell you exactly what time you are going to face death unless they are going to end your life for you. So why would we not choose to celebrate the gift of life until the very end. Do not misunderstand me, I fully understand that living with cancer is going to be a roller coaster of a ride because believe me I lived that experience with my son during the two years that we lived with cancer.

As an example, as difficult as it was to watch Rashard lose his speech we continued to find ways to combat this loss and navigate our way around this obstacle; such as using pen and paper or Rashard's phone and hand held device so that he could write down his needs and continue to communicate. Ironically, it was the gift of Rashard's hands that he had grown to rely on daily on the tennis court, that he turned to communicate with us when the brain tumour impeded on his ability to communicate through speech.

You know that old saying, "where there is a will there is a way." Even when Rashard could no longer use electronic devices to communicate we still continued to communicate in a way in which we understood each other. We eventually got to the stage where communication could only be done in silence. It was probably at this point that I truly understood the power of silent communication. My son knew that I loved him, and I knew that he loved me, even without words or conversation. Not only did I come to understand the power of non-verbal communication with Rashard, but increasingly I came to know the power of non-verbal communication through prayer.

QUESTIONS:

Have you ever had an experience of God communicating and speaking to you through another person?

Can you recall a message that God has sent you through someone else?

Do you understand the need for faith to supersede vision?

Have you ever been faced with a situation or experience whereby you have had no alternative but to walk in faith?

REFLECTIONS

Chapter 10

HEALING HANDS AND FEATHERS

"Then we which are alive and remain shall be caught up together with them in the clouds, to meet the Lord in the air: and so, shall we ever be with the Lord." ~ 1 Thessalonians 4:17 [KJV]

Following Rashard's first round of radiotherapy, I was encouraged by my mum to go and spend some time at my Godmother's health clinic, to take a much-needed break and to spend some time with Rashard. It was also to introduce both Rashard and I to juicing and natural remedies to help make his body strong and to ensure that his body was being fed all of the nutrients needed. This would complement modern day medicine in an attempt to shrink the tumour. The entire week on the retreat was an experience in and of itself for all of us. You see Rashard from the start was adamant that he was not going to drink any of the juices, but I want to move along to share a spiritual experience that happened just before returning home.

After what felt like an extremely long week, I was given a massage and left in one of the treatment rooms to relax before making my way back over to the house, where Rashard was upstairs resting in our twin room waiting for me.

After the massage I lay down on the table in a completely relaxed state of mind. I can still vividly picture the entire layout and direction of the room that I was left to relax in. As I got up, stood at the foot of the massage table to leave, it was as though something took over my body. I started jumping up and down lightly on my toes before bowing and turning in different directions. Looking back, it almost reminds me of the type of rain dance you see growing up in Western movies. My body was clearly being guided to bow in certain directions and my arms and hands were being lifted up accordingly. As my body and spirit arrived back into the room, I walked from the foot of the bed towards the wall behind the top end of the bed, where my head had been resting during the massage. Hanging on the right-hand side of the wall was a tiny picture. I had not noticed the picture until that point, but I walked towards it and stared at it very closely. It was a modern-day picture depicting Jesus Christ. As I looked closely at the picture I could see a small, round, brightly glowing circle to the side of Jesus's head on the left-hand side. I did not really think much more into the picture, but I remember getting lost in the picture and the glowing circle registering itself into my mind. I turned to leave the room to make my way back over to the house.

As I left the room and closed the door, I turned to look up at the sky, but I could not look up directly, as the sun was beaming down directly on me. As I continued to look up at what was one of the brightest of clear blue skies I had ever seen, I had the most amazing experience. There were two baby birds flying above me to the left, and suddenly what appeared to be a baby golden feather, illuminated by the sun came tumbling down towards me out of the sky, it landed right next to the black walnut tree. I did not know at the time, but with later research came to understand that the black walnut tree in the natural health world depicts the brain. If you look closely the structure actually resembles the human brain. The walnut is considered one of the best foods for brain health.

With a squinting eye, I carefully tracked the feather as it tumbled, until the point of landing. It was immediately clear that this was a gift and something special that I needed to pick up. In my mind I wondered who the tiny birds represented, who was watching over me and what had they sent? I don't know why, but my mind always wanders to Carol when I think of this point of the experience. During my childhood Carol was like a second mother to me. I picked up the feather, which I still have to this day, and wandered back over to the house. I walked into the room that Rashard and I shared and had him sit up on the bed. I started to rub my hands together, sliding them back and forth until they were literally on fire. I held

73

my hands over Rashard's ears, almost cupping his head and I repeated the process of rubbing my hands together until the point of fire and then placing them over Rashard's ears continuously. Rashard obliged and engaged in my actions without any question, he just sat silently letting me do what I needed to do. I start to do a winding motion by the right side of his left ear and then a movement with my hand, as though I was pulling something out. This went on for a long time. Rashard and I just relaxed in our room after that, no further conversation required.

FEATHERS:

The biggest feather that has ever appeared, used by Rashard to show me his presence, was in February 2018. It was my first trip back to Florida since both Rashard and my dad passing. I was in Orlando for a week with my eldest son Kaleed. This visit was the first time my sister Mary and I had seen each other in person since Rashard passing. It was a very special day because Mary, based in Florida, drove hours from Coral Springs to Orlando for us to catch up and spend some time together. On this particular day we had been sitting by the pool talking for hours about life, our families and the whole experience from start to finish of losing Rashard. It was not the hottest of days in Florida as it was the beginning of February, but it was hot enough, especially coming from London, England for us to sit out by the pool in shorts and a vest top.

It was such a special day, anytime Mary and I are in the same space we can literally talk for hours. At the end of our conversation, Mary had to pack up and head back home to her children. I walked Mary to her car, and we said our goodbyes. I headed back to the pool side with Kaleed, who had come down from the hotel room to say goodbye to Mary. As I sat back on the sun lounger and looked up into a clear blue sky, suddenly out of nowhere appeared this big cloud in the shape of a feather. The feather cloud literally sat right above my head. I was shocked and in awe, I immediately knew that Rashard's spirit was present and that he was watching over us. The coolest and most remarkable thing about this experience was that I got to share it with Kaleed. Had he not been present in the moment, I am not sure if he would have understood the intensity and power in which God can visually depict presence. Kaleed, no doubt would have thought I was exaggerating, but the fact that he was sitting right next to me meant that the power of both God and Rashard's presence was undeniable.

"And when he had spoken these things, while they beheld, he was taken up; and a cloud received him out of sight." ~ Acts 1:9 [KJV]

"While he was still speaking, a bright cloud covered them, and a voice from the cloud said "This is my son, whom I love; with him I am well pleased. Listen to him." ~ Matthew 17:5 [NIV]

"And then shall they see the Son of man in a cloud with power and glory." ~ Luke21:27 [ESV]

REFLECTION:

Before Rashard passing I would often hear stories of ways in which loved ones communicate with their families after death. Some would say they find pennies, others would say feathers, or even hear bee sounds by their ears. For me Rashard will either come to me in my dreams or he will leave me feathers.

QUESTIONS:

Have you ever looked to the sky and said, " I know that was you God"?

Is there an object or sound that links you to your loved ones who have passed?

Can you remember specific occasions where these specific sights, sounds or objects presented? How was you left feeling?

I can vividly remember two occasions where feathers have presented in the sky that have true meaning and without a shadow of a doubt were 'God moments,' moments where God went above and beyond to let me know that He is at work. You know faith without sight is important, but when God communicates with you through sight, these moments are indeed powerful and special.

Has the Holy Spirit ever taken over your body?

DAILY REFLECTION TIPS:

I would like to encourage you to practice gratitude daily and as often throughout the day as possible. For some things that we might take for granted on a daily basis really do deserve a moment of gratitude. As an example, giving thanks upon opening our eyes in the morning is often overlooked. Not everyone who closes their eyes at night are fortunate enough to open them again in the morning.

No matter what, every evening we should be able to find something to be grateful for, even if it is just making it through that very day.

REFLECTIONS

REFLECTIONS

Chapter 11

THANK YOU

Thank you – "Expressing one's gratitude or thanks."

The simplest of thank-you is a great way to express gratitude. One of the most important things I have learnt in my life journey is that it is never too late to say thank you. Yes, it is good to thank people in the present moment, but there are certain life situations and experiences that do not always lead to an immediate thank you. Sometimes it can take minutes, hours, days, months or even years for us to understand and appreciate what can in fact be lost in the moment. It is important that when we do get those 'Aha' moments in which we realise the important roles that others play out in both the joyful and painful experiences in our lives, it is always relevant and important to go back and say thank you. Positive or negative, loving or painful learning experience, never disregard the importance of a simple thank you.

God places people in our lives at different stages of our journeys for both reason and purpose. We do not always need to know the reason or purpose, and we may not always immediately understand why we cross paths with those that we cross paths with, but rest assure we do not always need to know, nothing is by accident; through omniscience we are reminded that our God is an omnipresent God. True faith and trust does not require us to know or fully understand the reason behind events that take place in our lives. Remember our Maker already knows everything. We do not need to rely on our own understanding, when the time is right, He will always reveal to us what we need to know.

> *"Trust in the Lord with all your heart and lean not on your own understanding; in all your ways submit to him, and he will make your paths straight." ~ Proverbs 3:5-6 [NIV]*

My son Rashard led the way for reminding me of the importance of gratitude and always 'making' or if you prefer 'taking' the time to say thank you. Rashard reminded me of the importance of not only taking time to say thank you to those in our present, but the importance of remembering to take the time to go back and say thank you to those who we crossed paths with in our past.

> *"Give thanks in all circumstances; for this is the will of God in Christ Jesus for you." ~ 1 Thessalonians 5:18 [ESV]*

Rashard, as Rashard did, led by example. You see, when Rashard started to show signs of losing his speech, after a conversation I had with a dear friend, I decided that it would be a great idea to interview Rashard. I felt that this would be the best way to capture my son for exactly who he was in relation to both tennis and life. I also thought it would be a great opportunity for Rashard to share with his friends and family his experience of living with DIPG. I saw this as an opportunity to make an everlasting memory.

I had no idea of the depth, insight and level of thoughtfulness Rashard would give in relation to his tennis journey and experience of living with DIPG during the interview. Yes, from a very early age we were always aware that Rashard was 'wise beyond his years' but we were all well and truly touched, amazed and literally blown away by the level of maturity in which he responded when questioned. From the very start of the interview Rashard shared words of gratitude. He was very clearly able to express what his family, friends and coaches, who he had crossed paths with along the way, all meant to him. Not only did Rashard give us a great understanding of his life journey, but he also expressed gratitude for those who joined us on the 'Yellow Walk for Rashard' to support him through DIPG. It makes me smile to think about the fact that during the interview he revealed his secret tennis weapon as being his inside out down the line forehand. He of course shared this revelation with one of his cheeky grins.

The biggest thank you, that to this day still stands out in my mind, is the reply given when asked: "who was your favourite tennis coach?" Rashard immediately without too much thought answered "Valda". I paused for a moment because I did not immediately make the connection. It clearly was not the coach who I thought it would be, but when he went into detail and explained "Valda because if I didn't meet her I would not have played tennis," a light switch went on inside of my head. This response immediately teleported me back to the first day that Rashard ever played tennis on the Furzedown tennis courts. It was moving for me to hear Rashard recognise this coach in his interview, very clearly reminding us all that if it was not for her he would not have had the opportunity to play tennis. It makes me smile because like my 'Basketball Angels', I have come to the realise that Rashard himself had his very own 'Tennis Angels'.

My original idea was for me to interview Rashard, but I had not had any prior experience of interviewing another person, yet alone my dying son. My uncertainty of knowing how to put together interview questions led me to seek help from a producer called Emma. I had met Emma a few years prior to Rashard's diagnosis, around the time that he used to attend WJTI with Aliya. I remember the timeframe clearly because Emma and I had been working on a project together. In working together, we had conversations about our children. Emma herself had one son. From memory, he was many years younger than my own children.

In sharing stories about our children, I shared stories about Rashard and Aliya playing tennis; showing pictures and short video clips of them in their element on the tennis court. At the time I jokingly mentioned that Emma could produce a documentary on my children's journey through tennis once they made it. It was one of those 'many a true word is spoken in jest' moments.

The moment I reached out to Emma and explained that Rashard had been diagnosed with DIPG and was starting to show signs of rapid speech deterioration she immediately sprang into action. My initial contact with Emma, searching for support in writing interview questions, very quickly turned into Emma offering to give up her time and the time of a small crew to carry out Rashard's final interview professionally. "Donna do not worry, I will interview Rashard for you, all you need to do is get a location. I'll get a cameraman and soundman down so that we do it properly."

I knew that I could trust Emma with Rashard's interview because although under totally different circumstances, I had already had first-hand experience of the quality of work she produced. Emma was diligent in production just as Rashard was diligent on the tennis court; I immediately knew we were onto a winner. The only task Emma delegated to me for recording Rashard's video was to find a location. I previously mentioned God's faithfulness and the fact that He sends you an army and provides all that we need, very often without us even realising, well this is a perfect example.

We went from producing a home interview to something so much bigger.

I took my one task of finding a location seriously. My first and only port of call was a guy called Lee, the manager at the National Tennis Centre (NTC). Lee from early days was one of Rashard's 'Tennis Angels'. I cannot remember exactly how we meet him, but what I do recall is that on meeting we struck up a friendship that saw him become one of both Rashard and Aliya's biggest cheerleaders. You see Lee introduced a programme for disadvantaged children that would not otherwise have been able to access the NTC tennis centre. He was just a genuine and caring person who wanted nothing more than to provide the opportunity for children to play tennis regardless of background, social class, gender or race.

On receiving my call, not only did Lee agree to us filming Rashard's final interview at the NTC, but he decided he wanted to make the occasion more memorable for Rashard. It was the year that the GB men had won the Davis Cup. Taking a starring role in the Davis cup team was a young tennis player Kyle Edmund. Not only did Lee set up a time for us to record at the NTC, but in fact he set up a time that would incorporate Rashard being given the opportunity to meet Kyle Edmund and to view the Davis Cup that was on tour across the country. In fact, it was the last day that the Davis cup was on display at the NTC. On finishing introductions to Kyle and the initial start of the interview the Davis Cup was packed up and put in a van for the next stop of the tour.

One of the things that I remember most about Rashard meeting Kyle and his agent at the time, Frasier, was the care and compassion that they showed towards Rashard. Frasier even went so far as to take my number saying that we would have to come down and watch Kyle play sometime. What I thought at the time was a fleeting moment and gesture soon played out into something so much bigger and meaningful to Rashard. Literally within a matter of months later, there we were sitting in Kyle Edmund's box at Queens. What is more incredible is in fact the week leading up to Queens, Rashard took a turn for the worse. He literally had no strength to get up out of bed, but low and behold on that day we were to watch Kyle Edmund play, Rashard mustered up what can only be described as God given strength. Rashard sat in the box and intently watched every stroke of the ball and every point played.

"He gives strength to the weary and increases the power of the weak." ~ Isaiah 40:29 [NIV]

"But those who hope in the Lord will renew their strength. They will soar on wings like eagles; they will run and not grow weary; they will walk and not be faint." ~ Isaiah 40:31 [NIV]

The day of the interview is a day I will never forget. Standing behind the camera and listening to Rashard answer the questions that Emma had prepared filled me with admiration. It was the first time I had heard Rashard talk in such depth about his whole experience of being diagnosed with a brain tumour and what that meant to him. Rashard's answers to the questions came straight from the heart and every word that left his mouth touched me deeply. Rashard's level of thoughtfulness and maturity as he articulately answered Emma's questions left me feeling emotionally in awe.

To Emma, Ben, Taron, Lee, Kyle and Frasier, saying thank you will never be enough. We will be forever grateful for the joyful moments and memories you were able to create and capture from Rashard. We will always be grateful for your time that you so generously and lovingly gave. In fact, in writing this thank you, I am reminded of a message that Taron aka 'The Soundman' sent to me the day after the interview.

In summary the message simply and eloquently summed up the invaluable luxury of time and the importance of never becoming too busy that we do not share it with those that are dear to us. In a message Taron so simply stated:

"Rashers is an example of courage in the face of adversity to us all. I came away quite moved by some of his comments, and as a father I changed my plans to stay in London and returned to my family to spend valuable time that we forget we have the luxury of."

QUESTIONS:

Do you actively practice gratitude through saying thank you?

Is there someone that stands out in your mind that you feel the need to say thank you to, who you may not previously have had the opportunity to say thank you to?

Has God ever sent you an army to support you to achieve something greater than you ever thought you could achieve?

REFLECTIONS

REFLECTIONS

Chapter 12

GOODBYE FOR NOW & CELEBRATING LIFE

Celebration: "The action of celebrating an important day or event."

Life: "The period between birth and death, or the experience or state of being alive."

GOODBYE:

No matter how you look at it, it is never easy to say goodbye to a loved one but saying goodbye to your child due to an incurable illness can be described as more debilitating than any other final goodbye. I say this based on the fact that we naturally expect children to outlive the lives of their parents.

To watch your healthy, strong child slowly wither away into a body of which they lose total control, while still fully aware of the world that exists around them, I can only describe, in and of itself, as a whole different level of experience.

If I search for goods news in the lead up to saying goodbye it leads me to the video interview of Rashard at the NTC. This being because it was the last opportunity we had to capture Rashard sharing his experience of tennis and living with DIPG on camera. Thinking back, the ability to record Rashard's final words in the lead up to him passing is incredible. To hear him share real meaningful thought and experiences on camera gave us all further insight into his being.

To hear Rashard voice his perspective at the end on life, moving from initially saying, "I'm not ready to die because I still have so much left to do with my life," to "I am ready to die mum because I can't do what I need to do here," completely changed my perspective on letting go and saying goodbye.

Rashard's departure gave me some insight into the realm beyond life. Rashard's conversations led me to believe that he had been to see what the journey or world he was going to transition into, once leaving this world, would be like. To hear my dying son confidently tell me "it is ok mum, I am still going to win tennis championships on the big tennis court up there in the clouds." Is mind blowing.

CELEBRATION OF LIFE:

It was not by accident that I chose to hold the celebration of Rashard's life on the day of my birthday, August 11th. At the time of making this decision, I had in my mind concluded that this would be my final opportunity to create one last special bond between us. I will always celebrate Rashard's life on my birthday.

With growth and development, I now feel that God may have guided me to this day because through the death of His son Jesus we get to celebrate and experience eternal life. I myself was blessed to have had the opportunity to experience the feeling of celebrating the life of my son first-hand. A day that will remain in my heart forever. Some may wonder how on earth I arrived at this interpretation.

The lead up to the day in which we came together with friends and family to celebrate Rashard's life was pretty hectic. Right up to the evening before we were up late putting together the last of the programmes. I smile because even in putting together the programmes God sent me a living Angel in Corrine, I give all credit to the final programme to Corinne. I was so tired that during that day I could no longer think straight to get the page layout right for everything to be sent over to the printer, but along came Corinne to take charge and ensure that like everything else, the programmes were perfect. I wanted to make Rashard proud by giving him a final send-off worthy of the gift that he was to all of us. A send-off as perfect as celebrating the passing of my son could be.

Prior to passing, Rashard expressed his final wishes very clearly. He told us that he wanted to be cremated and that he wanted his ashes to be brought home. In preparing for Rashard's funeral, there was a moment in which I paused and pondered on whether or not I should instead go with a burial. I was quickly reminded by friends and family that I should definitely honour Rashard's wishes and go with the cremation, after all Rashard had been very vocal in expressing his wishes throughout the whole experience of living with DIPG. He had also shared his wish to be cremated with Laura, his palliative care nurse.

I was very meticulous in the planning of Rashard's Celebration of Life. I was super conscious that there would be many of Rashard's school and tennis friends present. For many this would be there first real experience of the passing of a friend. I wanted everyone to be able to express their sadness, but at the same time I wanted them to remember Rashard with fondness. I did not want any feeling of sombreness looming in the air. It is funny because I can remember going to make the final service arrangements with the vicar. He was adamant that the organ needed to be played because it was a funeral, but in my mind the sound of the organ would ring solemnness and sadness. Do not misunderstand me, of course the day was going to be sad, but we just did not need to let the tones of death ring throughout the service. The celebration of life needed to be representative of Rashard and who he was. This meant that we had to include the things that were important to him – family, friends and most importantly, tennis.

The fact that tennis was Rashard's everything meant that we needed to pay one last visit to Wimbledon. With Rashard's body carefully resting inside of his coffin, he was carefully drawn up a hill in a carriage by four beautiful, big, strong black horses to Wimbledon Centre Court. Rashard's name was spelt out in the most perfect big bold yellow roses. This floral arrangement being a gift from one of his Dad's best friends, Jimmy. This detail as we took route on the final walk before the church service was perfect. Rashard himself very precise and meticulous I know was smiling over us, for he had a final walk that was fit for a King. He will forever be remembered as our 'King of the Court'. The roads up to Wimbledon were airily clear. It was as though God ensured the roads ahead were clear every step of the way. As we reached Wimbledon Centre Court the horses and carriage paused. I got out of the limousine and approached the carriage to have a few final words with my son Rashard. Wimbledon was familiar for Rashard because he had, prior to joining Tennis Avenue, been on the WJTI Squad. Taking the route past Wimbledon was important, especially because in parting Rashard had said *"don't worry Mum I can still win Championships on that big tennis court up there in the clouds."* I wanted Rashard to know that we still had faith that he could achieve all that he planned to achieve, only now he would continue to play tennis in Heaven. Centre Court at Wimbledon I would describe as Rashard's Heaven on Earth. Only now Rashard was leaving us to experience something very special. He was about to enter Heaven and play tennis on the King of all Tennis Courts. I feel proud and an element of awe when I think about what Rashard must be doing on the big tennis court up there in the clouds. In my heart I know he is working hard, after all that was the final message he left to all of his family and friends, "Work Hard."

After the final procession we arrived at the church, Rashard's coffin carefully taken out of the carriage. The coffin itself was beautiful. It was solid matt black with silver fittings. His coffin had been custom-made. The bold yellow rose spray that covered Rashard's coffin popped off against the black background. Rashard's Dad, older brother Kaleed and cousins carried his coffin into the church; in front of them walked his younger brother Shareef carrying another beautiful floral arrangement, made up in the shape of a tennis racket. As they carried Rashard down the aisle to the front of the church the Donny Hathaway version of the song 'Young Gifted and Black' played in the background. It was one of my best friends Cheryl who had selected this specific song and the moment I heard it I knew that this song needed to be played as Rashard was carried into the church. For he was the epitome of that song, young, gifted and black.

The service itself was beautiful. God filled me with a strength to stand strong and tall to address the crowd of over four hundred friends and family that filled the church. I delivered Rashard's Eulogy with great pride.

God stood by my side and filled me with the strength and words needed to address the crowd and share a message of hope and encouragement. My aim being to send a clear message to Rashard's young friends, our friends and our family that through death we get to celebrate life. A message of hope and encouragement

> *"But the Lord stood at my side and gave me strength, so that through me the message might be fully proclaimed, and all the Gentiles might hear: And I was delivered from the lion's mouth." ~ 2 Timothy 4:17 [NIV]*

The entire service was of thanksgiving to celebrate the beautiful gift of life. It was not only to celebrate Rashard's life, but a great reminder for all present to be grateful for God's gift of life and through Rashard be reminded of God's promise of everlasting love and eternal life.

Rashard's body leaving the church grounds was an experience in itself. Rashard's friends, young tennis players with dreams of their own lined both sides of the path on which the beautiful horse drawn carriage made its exit. They stood in silence with their tennis rackets stretched above them forming a guard of honour, all wearing their bright yellow 'Work Hard for Rashard' t-shirts. I always pause and smile when I picture

Rashard's friends forming the guard of honour because it was incredible.

> *"For God so loved the world that he gave His only begotten Son, that whoever believes in Him shall not perish but have everlasting life." ~ John 3:16 [NKJV]*

QUESTIONS:

Have you ever been given insight into life beyond death?

How have you said goodbye to your love ones?

How do you honour the memory of your loved ones?

How often do you take time to pause and remember your loved ones that have passed?

REFLECTIONS

Chapter 13

SPREADING THE WORD

God led me back to Idaho. I was not sure exactly why God was taking me back to Nampa, Idaho again, but true to His way He chose to use the guise of basketball to lead me there, just one more time. Only this time God was not leading me into the wilderness, but I believe showing me the way out. I was so close to finding my way out, but God wanted to literally hold my hand as I approached and made my way down the final stretch towards the brightest of lights that would lead me to my final calling. I knew from the moment my sister Mary sent me a simple message stating, "we need to go to this" with the flyer attached to the message, that an incredible shift was about to take place in my life and true to my feeling, that is exactly what happened.

It's funny because the time between receiving the message from Mary in May and leaving for the trip in November, the days went by so quickly. In the lead up to the event my teammates started to make arrangements, booking tickets and places to stay for the homecoming event. What they did not know is that I had not booked my ticket or thought about where I was going to stay when in Idaho because in my mind God had already spoken to my heart to confirm who I needed to spend time with.

The end of August I started to communicate with one of my 'Basketball Angels' Dave Whittinger. You see I met Dave, his wife Twila and their children during my Sophomore year at NNU. They were my 'Crusader Family'. Unfortunately, Twila passed away from a tumour herself in December 2017.

Dave and I began to communicate and talk about our families and how our children had grown and were moving through life. We instantly reconnected and I began to really look forward to being able to sit down with Dave to share some of our life experiences. The biggest conversations I knew we would have, would be in relation to having to say goodbye to our loved ones. For Dave, the passing of his wife Twila, and for me, the passing of my son Rashard.

I confirmed with Dave that I would love to take up his offer to stay at his home during my visit. For some reason I knew this was exactly where I was going to stay even before the offer was made. It is funny because I did not feel nervous or hesitant about staying at Dave's home because he, despite the years since last seeing him, is like family to me. I simply followed God's direction and stayed where he intended me to be.

Walking through the airport at Boise Idaho, I paused and asked myself "how did I end up back here?" It was a surreal moment, but one that I fully understood. I already knew the answer to the question that I paused to ask myself. You see this visit was going to be about so much more than returning to NNU for Homecoming, basketball and to celebrate 50 Years of Women in Sport. For me I had this deeply seated feeling that this journey was going to be about acknowledgement, revelation, spiritual development and growth. This trip was almost some type of confirmation that I had successfully survived my mission and God was going to affirm this by reconnecting me with some of the key people that I crossed paths with during the early period of my wilderness experience. It was like connecting up dots from some twenty plus years ago.

The moment I touched down at Boise and walked through the airport I had this sense of returning home. Never would I have ever thought that returning to Idaho would feel like home, but it did. My return to Idaho immediately revealed advancement. The place I once knew as remote and isolated was no longer so, it had become a city enriched through development and growth, very similar to how I felt as a person. It is hard to know exactly how to describe the feeling, but my arrival to Idaho gave me an immediate sense of achievement and accomplishment. A feeling of peace and tranquillity immediately swept over me. I had not felt such a level of peace and ease since Rashard's death.

My arrival to Idaho filled me with gratitude. I was about to be reunited with coaches, teammates and friends that I last came into contact with twenty-eight years ago, this included a friend of mine called Govai, who treated me like a sister on my initial arrival to Idaho to 'play basketball'. God was about to take me on a journey to recap my walk-through life from the point of me arriving in Idaho for my freshman year to me returning decades later to celebrate 'homecoming'.

God's faithfulness meant that he directed me to the perfect person to sit with, reflect on and explore my entire experience. He led me to a living Angel that would not only be able to discuss the trials and tribulations of my journey, but he sent me a person that would help me to identify and reflect on all of the shining experiences of my journey, experiences worthy of celebration and praise. I would say the biggest celebrations were that of being blessed with four beautiful children, a blessing that I do not take lightly.

From the day I set foot inside Dave's home I felt a sense of complete freedom. We would sit down and visit each other as though we had seen each other regularly across the years. We enjoyed exchanging stories of our experiences of caring for our loved ones and saying goodbye. It was during these moments that I was able to share through reflection my experience of basketball during my time at NNU.

During day to day reflection time and conversation with Dave, God began to really reveal to me the purpose of my visit, of which on this occasion, I knew was about more than just basketball. He used this time to revisit some of my more painful wilderness experiences in a safe and isolated way. Dave and I would wake up early every morning and sit down and chat for a couple hours over hot drinks. I really valued the time that we spent talking. Our conversation just flowed with ease. We discussed the tough times experienced through the wilderness, but we also discussed and shone light on the good times. One thing that I felt strongly during our discussions was that I was so close and on the edge of coming out of the wilderness. I would describe this feeling of coming out of the wilderness very similar to the one that I had going in to the wilderness when I first arrived in Nampa Idaho. You know they say when people are dying, they see events that they have gone through flash before their eyes. Well for me it was as though God was revealing to me that I had successfully completed his mission, and that I was about to transition to another level of which was about to allow me to experience something completely different in this lifetime. My deliverance would now see me ready to come out and share my experience by bearing witness to God's faithfulness to those who choose to trust in and follow Him.

"Ask, and it will be given to you; Seek and you will find: knock, and it shall be opened to you." ~ Matthew 7:7 [ESV]

QUESTION:

Have you ever been guided to a location or can you identify a point or moment in time in your life where you have had the opportunity to reflect on your journey through life?

REFLECTIONS

Chapter 14

SELF, OTHERS AND GOD

Self: "The self is an individual person as the object
of its own reflective consciousness."

Others: "Denoting a person or thing that is different or
distinct from one already mentioned
or known about."

God: "God is usually conceived as being Omniscience
(all-knowing), Omnipotent (all powerful),
Omnipresent (all present)."

Days after arriving in Idaho and catching up with
friends and teammates, I found myself sitting in Coach
Schmidt's barn with some of my teammates, this gave me the
opportunity I had been waiting for. An opportunity to say
thank you to one of God's biggest 'Prayer Warriors' and one
of my 'Basketball Angels'. The opportunity to say thank you
to my coach in person was pretty incredible. Imagine sitting

amongst a servant who had for many years delivered God's word and teaching under the title of Basketball Coach. This was one of my biggest 'Aha' moments if ever I had one. This moment was pretty incredible for me, one that I truly believe and foresee as a turning point for me, not just in my adult life, but in completing a mission and being carefully guided out of the wilderness. This trip to Nampa, Idaho and this opportunity to say thank you was both a teaching and learning experience for me. Everything in my life and my experience of surviving the DIPG journey finally all made sense. I can only describe the opportunity to go on this trip as a revelation to me.

A revelation to me of the initial reason behind me being teleported to Nampa, Idaho at the age of nineteen; my soul being stripped back and filled with the Holy Spirit under the guidance of God's messengers. God's teachings and scattering of seeds through Coach Schmidt and Coach Ely had blossomed and here I was standing tall as an example of the fruits that bear out of trust and faith. Consciously or unconsciously, the seeds that had scattered amongst God's children decades later proved to be fruitful. Although just a handful of fruit appeared in Coach Schmidt's barn that day, in the form of my basketball teammates, it only took that handful of all present to recognise and acknowledge how blessed we are to have been sowed in Nampa, Idaho during our teenage years. We returned not only as a handful of those seeds that had blossomed, but we were there as a representation of how the Word of God can spread thick and fast through many. We had all gone from seeds to blossom, to blooming and bearing fruit through our children and all of the adults and young people that we come into contact with daily as we walk through life. Who would have ever imagined that we, God's chosen ones, under the guise of basketball would be sent out amongst the people to spread His Word by leading and practicing virtues such as love, patience and kindness?

The very same evening of God providing me with the opportunity to give thanks over lunch, we attended the special homecoming dinner. It was at this moment that God took over my mouth and revealed to me three of the most important relationships he had taught me during my time as a student athlete at Northwest Nazarene University. God spoke to and through me. At the dinner there was a roaming mic. God took over my mind and my mouth. Through me he summarised the importance of three key relationships in life, the relationship to *Self*, the relationship to *Others* and last, but most importantly the relationship we develop with *God* (SOG). A way of thinking that I now plan to share through teaching and preaching; what I truly with all my heart believe is my calling.

Following my trip to Idaho, I returned home to London, England full. The Holy Spirit filled me up with a whole other level of Holy Spirit, if that even makes sense. I felt like I had been baptised into a whole new level of being. God's being. I returned to London, England with a strong sense and feeling that God would now use me to deliver what he had spent all of these years preparing me for. I returned to London openly proclaiming that I was ready to preach, share God's word and use what felt like my most 'challenging experiences' to share and deliver the Word of God. Every morning since my return to England, I lift my hands up and I say, "Here I am God, I am yours, I give my life over to you completely." Words cannot even begin to express the level of excitement that fills me.

I needed to return to Idaho for some type of epiphany into what was next for me. For God to make clear to me what I will be sharing from the teaching and learning of this experience. In order for God to send me on my next mission, of which would be about celebrating life and fruitfulness, I truly needed to understand death. God gave me insight and vision into what lay ahead on the other side of my wilderness experience. Just thinking about experiencing my next level of life and what is to come fills my soul with a nervous and unsettled feelings of excitement, mixed with awe and wonder. This trip I feel, was the final leg of the original mission, but the start of something new. God choosing to reveal to me all that I needed to learn and all that I learnt in order to bring me closer to Him and worthy of preaching His message through leading and serving others. The time has arrived for me to go out and counsel others by sharing my experiences as a testimony to the awesomeness of God's word, believing and fully understanding that he sent His only Son into this world to save us. This journey I would classify as me finally succumbing to God's teachings and seeing the light. The 'Aha' moment of my spiritual journey has finally arrived.

"Declare His glory among nations, His wonders among all peoples." ~ Psalm 96:3 [NKJV]

I returned from my visit to Idaho with life making complete sense. I returned declaring that I was born to preach and share God's word through sharing our journey. So, I guess here is where the next stage of life's journey begins for me....

"The LORD is my light and my salvation; whom shall I fear? The LORD is the strength of my life; of whom shall I be afraid?" ~ Psalm 27-1 [NKJV]

QUESTIONS:

Do you have an experience or journey that you have been able to reflect on that you would like to share with friends and family or on a wider scale to show how you came to know and understand that your relationship with God is at the core of your being?

On a scale of 0 to 10 how much control do you believe you have had on events that have played and continue to play out in your life?

0	1	2	3	4	5	6	7	8	9	10

REFLECTIONS

REFLECTIONS

REFLECTIONS

REFLECTIONS

REFLECTIONS

Notes

Page 1: Oxford University Press (2019 reflection. In Lexico.com, Available at https://www.dictionary.com/browse/reflection?s=t [Accessed 28/05/2020].

Page 9: https://www.merriam-webster.com/dictionary/adversity [Accessed 28/05/2020].

Page 9: Oxford University Press (2019 resilience. In Lexico.com, Available at https://www.lexico.com/definition/resilience [Accessed 28/05/2020].

Page 17: https://www.gotquestions.org/wilderness-experience.html [Accessed 28/05/2020].

Page 17: Oxford University Press (2019 wonder. In Lexico.com, Available at https://www.lexico.com/definition/wonder [Accessed 28/05/2020].

Page 25: Oxford University Press (2019 angel. In Lexico.com, Available at https://www.lexico.com/definition/angel [Accessed 28/05/2020].

Page 31: Oxford University Press (2019 prayer. In Lexico.com, Available at https://www.lexico.com/definition/prayer [Accessed 28/05/2020].

Page 45: Oxford University Press (2019 predestined. In Lexico.com, Available at https://www.lexico.com/definition/predestined [Accessed 28/05/2020].

Page 45: Oxford University Press (2019 premonition. In Lexico.com, Available at https://www.lexico.com/definition/premonition [Accessed 28/05/2020].

Page 55: Oxford University Press (2019 dream. In Lexico.com, Available at https://www.lexico.com/definition/dream [Accessed 28/05/2020].

Page 81: https://www.dictionary.com/browse/thank--you [Accessed 28/05/2020].

Page 93: Oxford University Press (2019 celebration. In Lexico.com, Available at https://www.lexico.com/definition/celebration [Accessed 28/05/2020].

Page 93: https://dictionary.cambridge.org/dictionary/english/life [Accessed 28/05/2020].

Page 111: https://en.wikipedia.org/wiki/Self [Accessed 28/05/2020].

Page 111: Oxford University Press (2019 other. In Lexico.com, Available at https://www.lexico.com/definition/other [Accessed 28/05/2020].

Page 111: https://en.wikipedia.org/wiki/God [Accessed 28/05/2020].